Jomi The Reporter

Sol | Publishing

KJV Bible

Graphic Art by Sol|Publishing

Copyright © 2018

Author Jomari K Moreno & Author Solmary Alicea

All rights reserved.

ISBN-13: 978-1987713008

YOU ARE AWESOME   YOU ARE BEAUTIFUL   YOU ARE CHOSEN

Jomi The REPORTER

YOU ARE AWESOME   YOU ARE BEAUTIFUL   YOU ARE CHOSEN

Jomi The Reporter

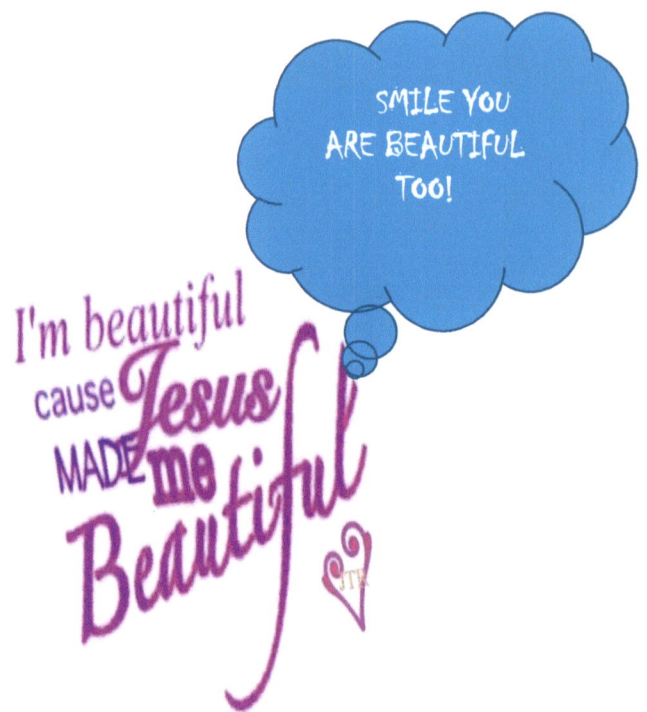

YOU ARE AWESOME   YOU ARE BEAUTIFUL   YOU ARE CHOSEN

4

JOMI MORNING
CHAPTER 1

The alarm clock rang, and Jomi stretched out from her bed, holding on tight to her mic.

"Jomi what are you holding?"

Her mother shouted down the hallway, but Jomi was too tired to listen.

She made it to the restroom before her little brother wakes up.

Her pink glittery mic clock said 10:07am. Eight minutes until Ziki her little brother alarm clock rings and until mother leaves to work.

Jomi turned around, opening the bathroom door looking for her little brother. When she squinted, she was pretty sure she saw him laying on his bed, with his little feet, surrounded with goodies and wrapper that he sneaked at night as mother was asleep.

"Ziki!" Jomi yelled on her mic.

Ziki looked up, went under his covers as he slides off the bed, and walked towards her as he rubs his eyes. When he got to her he was yawning.

"I'm tired! What do you want Jomi?" With his tire squeaky morning voice, he replies.

Jomi loves her little brother so much, but Ziki was not in a good mood to be bother. He is awesome with a lot of things but not when he wakes up especially when Jomi yells out aloud to wake him.

"How many minutes do we have?" Jomi asked, giggling as she holds her glittery mic up close to him.

"it's time for STRAWBERRY PANCAKES and CHOCOLATE MILK!" Ziki screamed with excitement as he ran almost to the stairs.

"STOOOP!"

Jomi yelled, 'silly Ziki you forgot to brush your teeth." She said.

Jomi grabbed Ziki by his hand to take him to wash his teeth.

"Good job Ziki now go ahead and enjoy yourself some delicious strawberry pancakes with some chocolate milk that mother prepared for you," said Jomi.

Ziki gave her a BIG THUMBS UP as he walked quickly down the stairs to eat his delicious strawberry pancakes with chocolate milk.

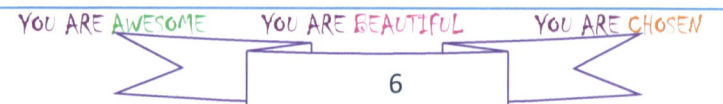

IT STARTS WITH YOU

CHAPTER 2

Auntie Denisse arrive to the house, to watch over Jomi and Ziki as their mother heads to work.

"Auntieeee!" Jomi and Ziki yelled with excitement as they ran towards her.

"HELLO, my babies" auntie replied, "Good Morning!'

"Auntie are you ready?" Jomi asked curiously.

"Well of course I am, a promise is a promise and I'm ready to go." The plan is to take JOmi and Ziki to the park that afternoon.

"Yesss!" Ziki screamed with joy, as he ran to get his shoes on with his matching orange hat.

Auntie Denisse walked with Jomi and Ziki two blocks down from their house to the park.

"You guys know the rules," Auntie said, "holding hands and looking both ways before crossing the street."

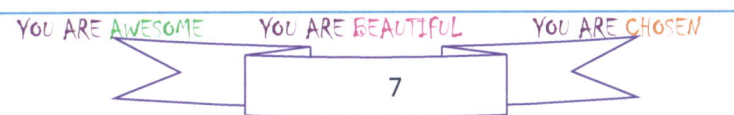

Jomi and Ziki grab hands and walked in front of their auntie as she follows from behind.

"We are here now!" Auntie said, as she lays the blanket on the green grass.

"Auntie, why is there so much papers around the swing set?" Jomi ask, as she wonder.

"Well, Jomi is sad to say that there are people that don't know any better, but you know what, let's make a difference and do better," said Auntie Denisse, "let's go pick up all those papers, bottles, and throw them inside those dumpsters right next to the fence."

So Jomi started cleaning up with her little brother and her with Auntie too.

"Auntie, when we get back home I'm going to do a report about this," said Jomi with a smile, "this is good to tell my friends at school to help out to keep our community shinning and clean!"

Auntie smiled and after picking up all the trash around the park Auntie Denisse was so proud of them, she took them for a treat.

"Ice Scream!" they all yelled out aloud as they walked across the street of the park.

"thank you, Auntie," Jomi said, "ROCK on Auntie Dee," as Ziki said with his giggling voice.

So off they go skipping back home.

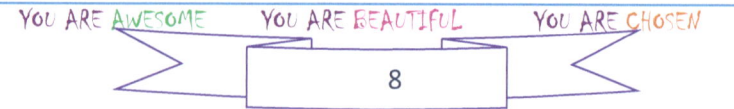

Jomi The Reporter

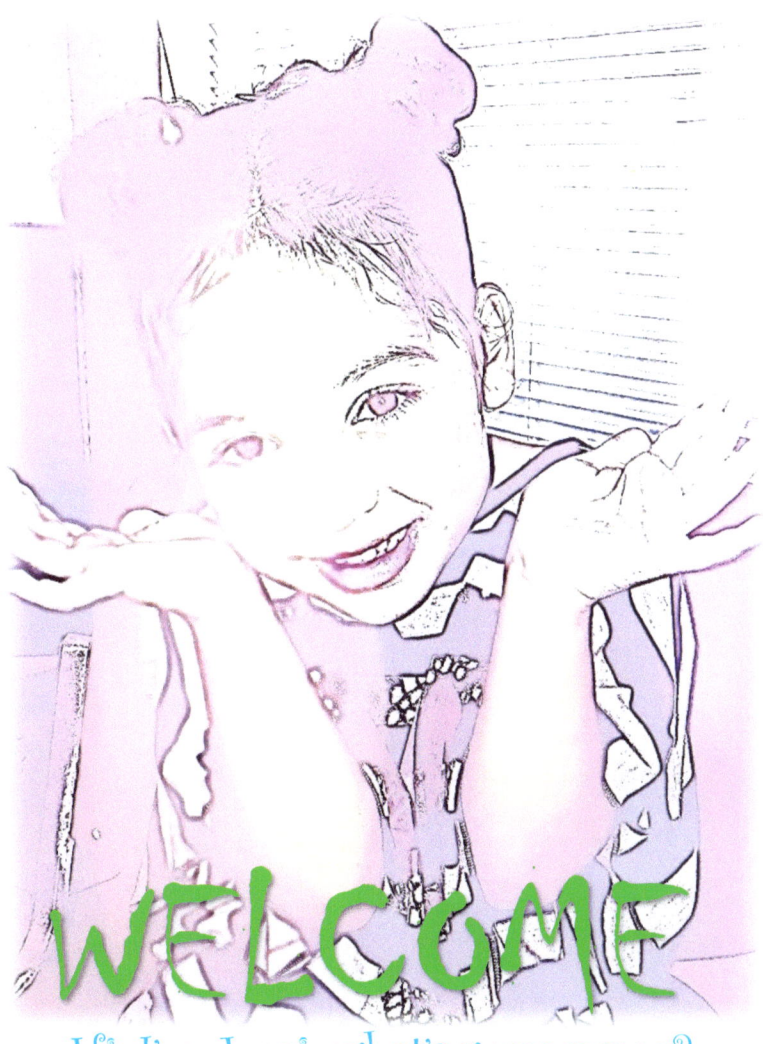

WELCOME

Hi, I'm Jomi, what's your name?

YOU ARE AWESOME   YOU ARE BEAUTIFUL   YOU ARE CHOSEN

9

Jomi The Reporter

Write a REPORT:

STEP 1: Draw a park that you would like to go to.

STEP 2: Draw a dumpster or a recycling bin.

STEP 3: Draw or write down on the bottom of the page stuff that you fine at the park that doesn't belong there.

STEP 4: Draw how you would make a difference on the park. (Use the other page if you have to.)

YOU ARE AWESOME   YOU ARE BEAUTIFUL   YOU ARE CHOSEN

10

Jomi The Reporter

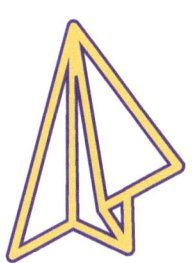

YOU ARE AWESOME   YOU ARE BEAUTIFUL   YOU ARE CHOSEN

11

Jomi The Reporter

Find Your Favorites Reports

My sister, Jomi, have made different kinds of reports, in this book. Use the puzzles to solve this jigsaw pieces hidden on the pages.

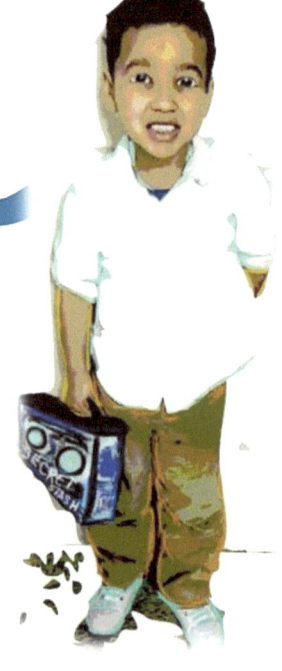

Each color makes a word:

GREEN

RED

ORANGE

BLUE

YELLOW

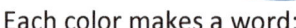

WRITE THE WORD

YOU ARE AWESOME   YOU ARE BEAUTIFUL   YOU ARE CHOSEN

12

Jomi The Reporter

RUN

HAVE FUN

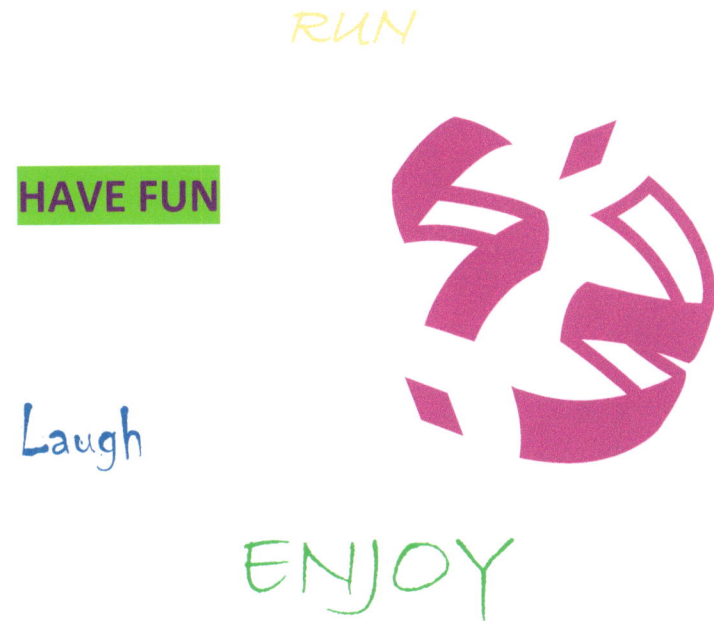

Laugh

ENJOY

BE A KID & KNOW LISTENING, FOLLOWING INSTRUCTIONS IS GOOD TOO.

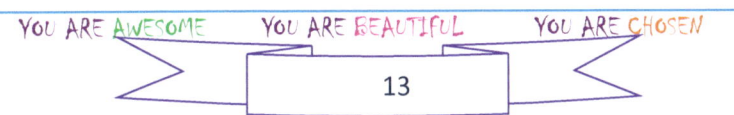

YOU ARE AWESOME   YOU ARE BEAUTIFUL   YOU ARE CHOSEN

13

Jomi The Reporter

Jomi has a friend named Toni

Toni's best friend is Jomi

If Jomi & Toni get lonely

Who would be their HOMIE?

Stand in front of the mirror and do this

 so, who is it?

YOU ARE AWESOME   YOU ARE BEAUTIFUL   YOU ARE CHOSEN

Jomi The Reporter

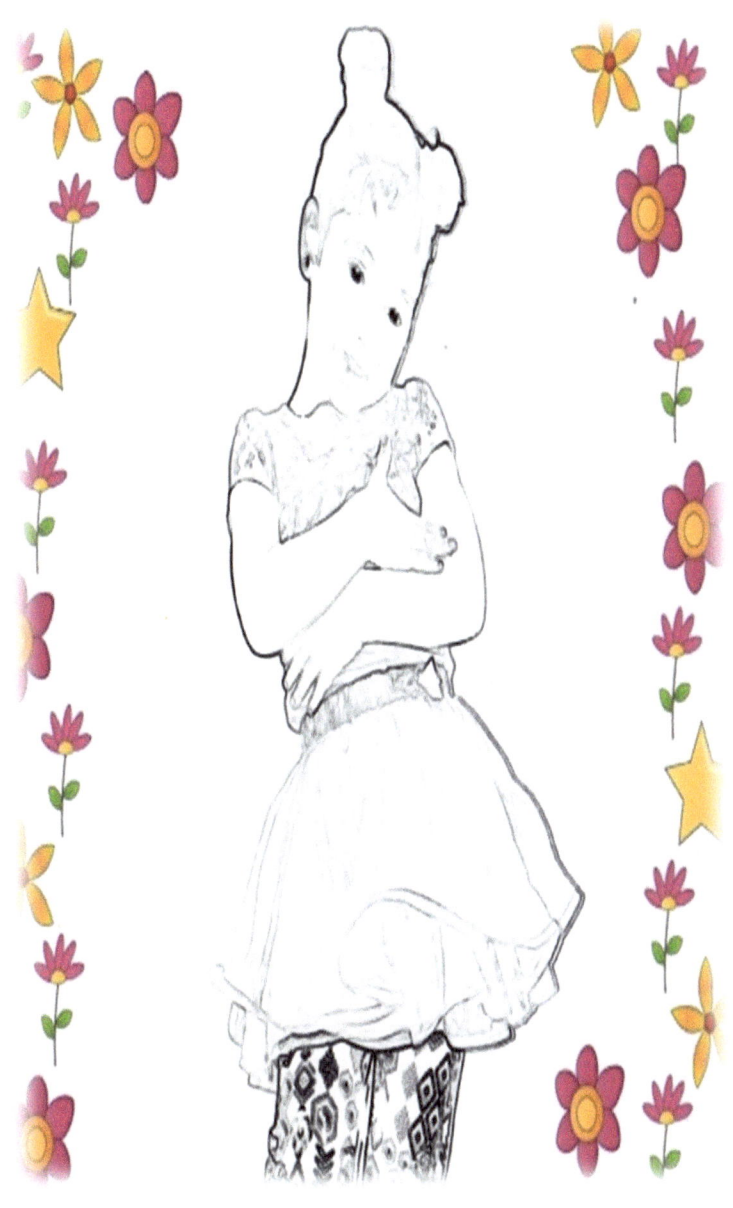

YOU ARE AWESOME   YOU ARE BEAUTIFUL   YOU ARE CHOSEN

15

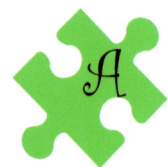

Little Ziki, likes to creep,

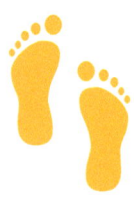

Tip Toe on his FEET,

To go find him a treat,

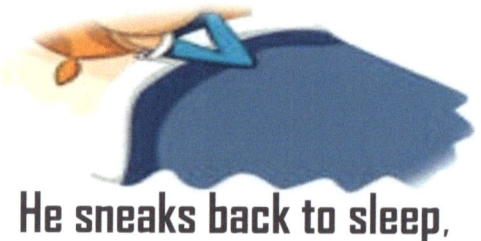

He sneaks back to sleep,

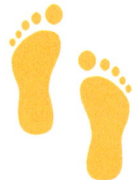

Jomi The Reporter

With food by his feet,

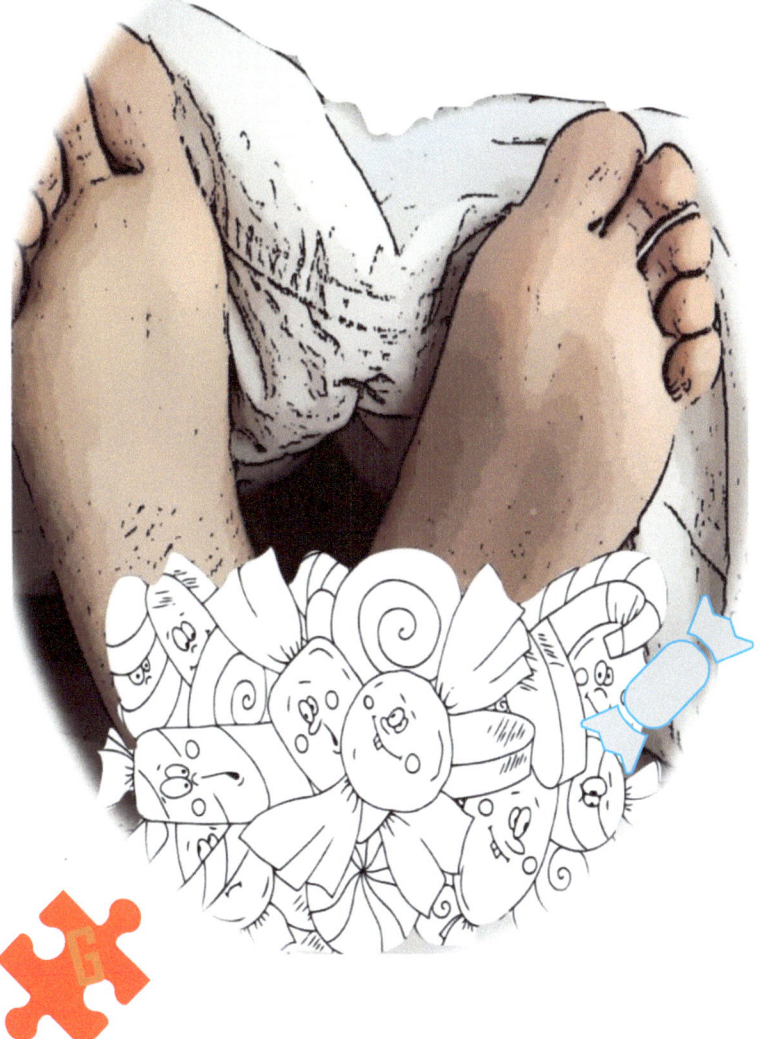

YOU ARE AWESOME   YOU ARE BEAUTIFUL   YOU ARE CHOSEN

17

Jomi The Reporter

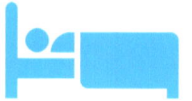

His mom is asleep

While he is a cheat, sneaking those goodies,

In his tummy they sleep

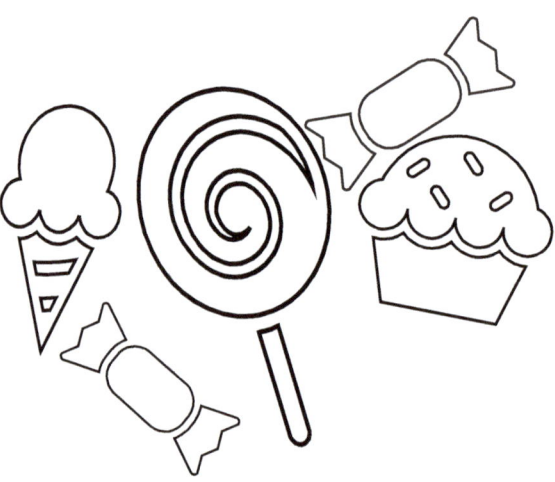

YOU ARE AWESOME   YOU ARE BEAUTIFUL   YOU ARE CHOSEN

Have some fun and color me too!

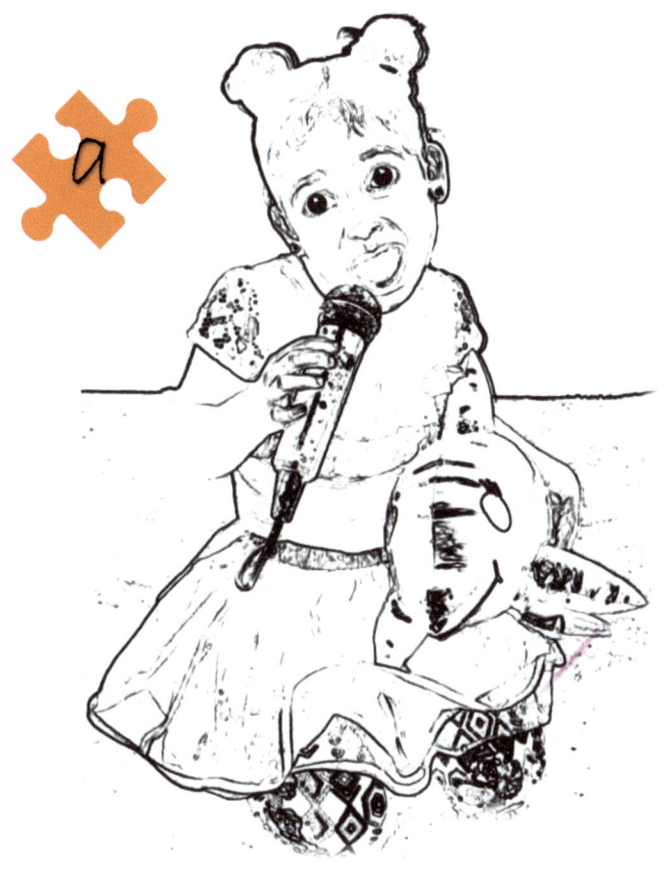

Jomi The Reporter

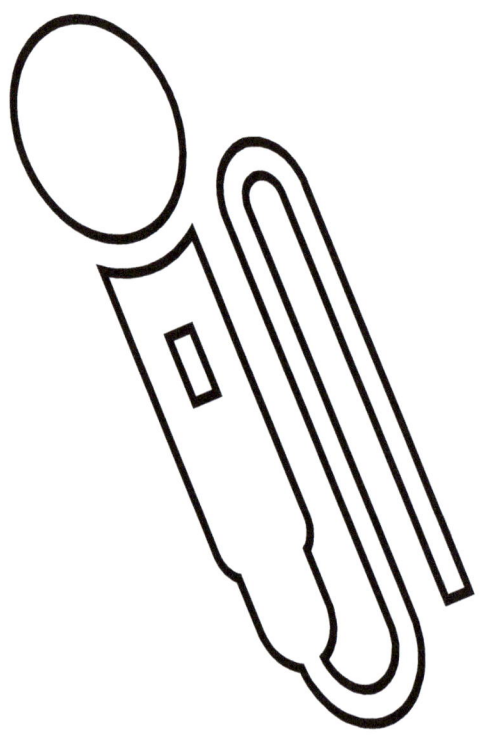

GO AHEAD COLOR YOUR MIC

YOU ARE AWESOME   YOU ARE BEAUTIFUL   YOU ARE CHOSEN

20

Jomi The Reporter

Certificate For The Most Awesome kid!

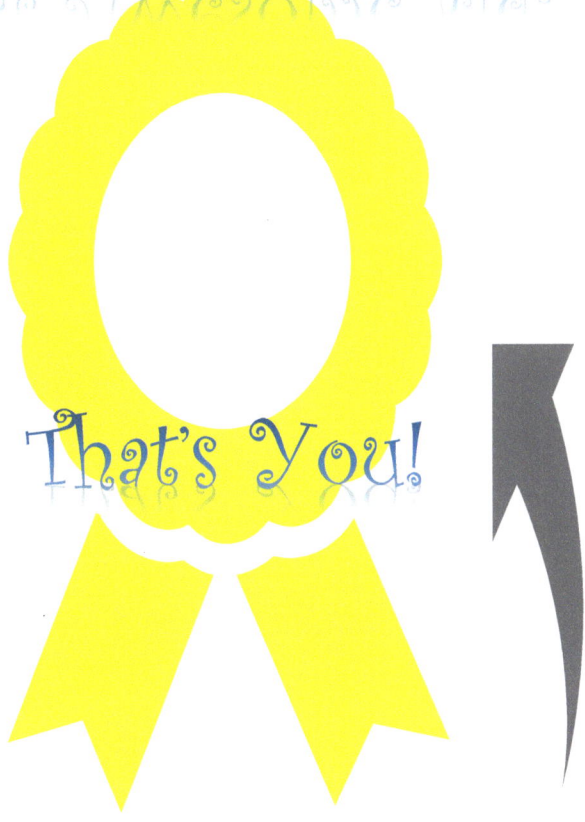

That's You!

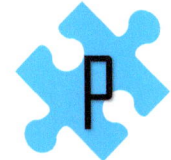

Draw a picture of You

YOU ARE AWESOME   YOU ARE BEAUTIFUL   YOU ARE CHOSEN

21

Jomi The Reporter

Jomi and Ziki think they are sneaky,

Pretending to go to sleep,

While their mom is in bed

They TIP TOE ahead,

And turn on the TV,

While their watching cartoons

They start laughing as soon,

As their mom gets on her feet,

They hear her footsteps as they

Run back to bed, pretending to

snore and sleep.

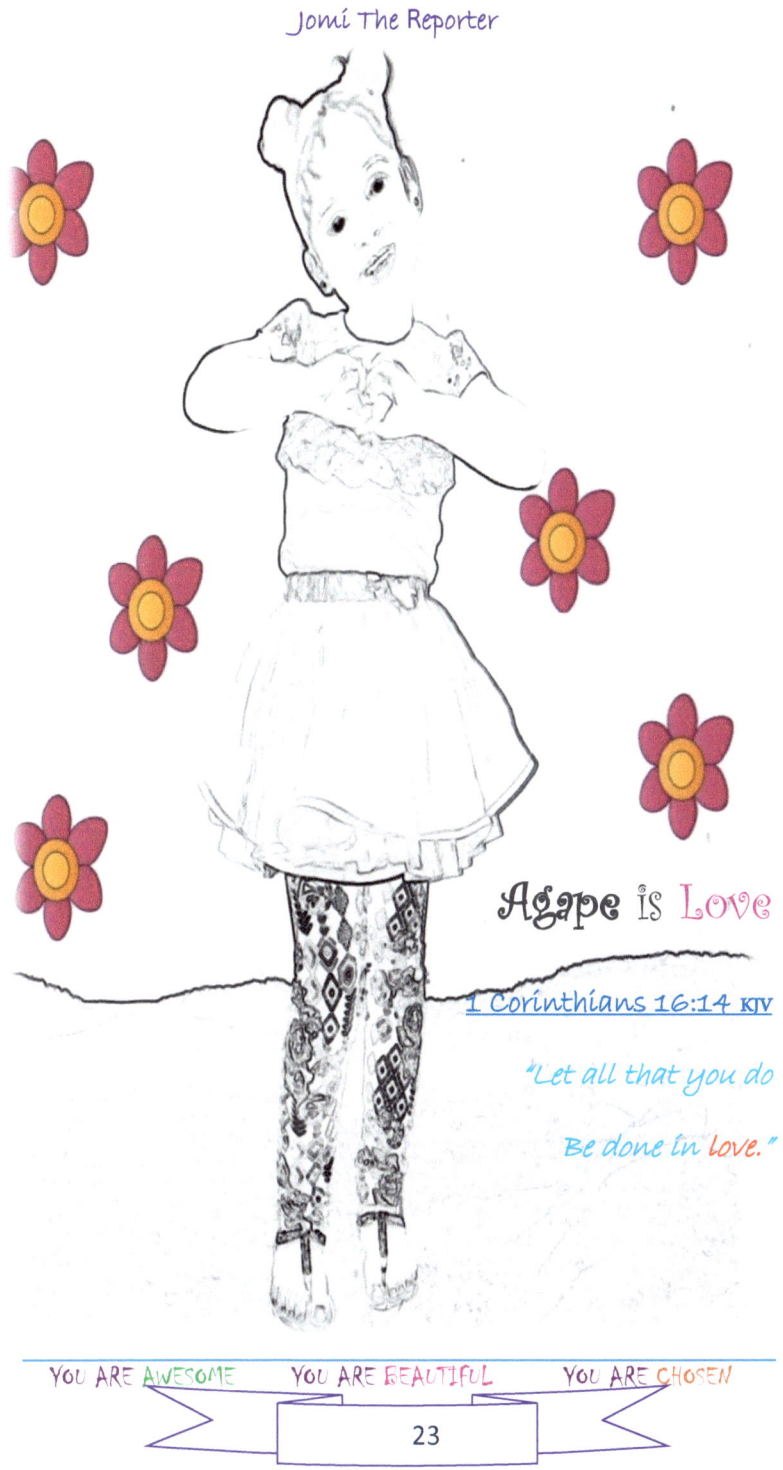

Jomi The Reporter

Draw your REPORT:

YOU ARE AWESOME YOU ARE BEAUTIFUL YOU ARE CHOSEN

24

Jomi The Reporter

Draw a line and match them.

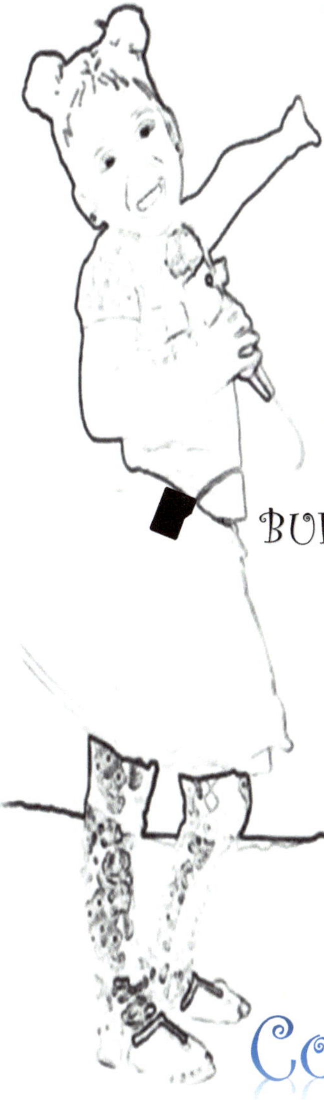

RADIO

SHOE

FEET

CAR

DRESS

BUILDING

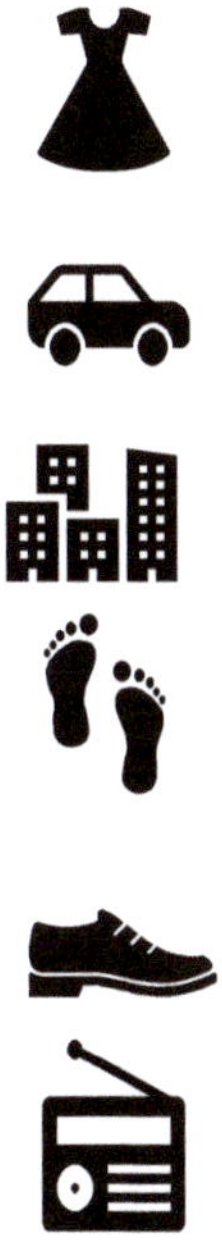

Color me too!

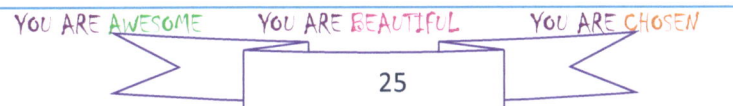

YOU ARE AWESOME   YOU ARE BEAUTIFUL   YOU ARE CHOSEN

25

Jomi The Reporter

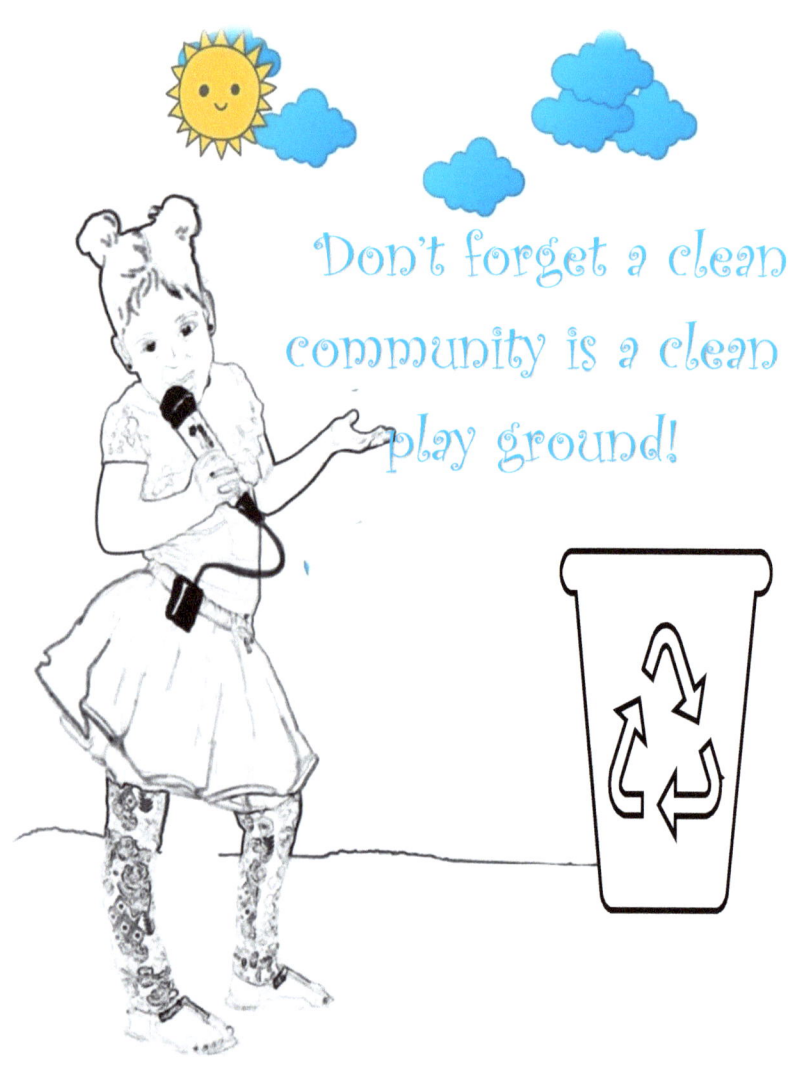

Don't forget a clean community is a clean play ground!

YOU ARE AWESOME   YOU ARE BEAUTIFUL   YOU ARE CHOSEN

Jomi The Reporter

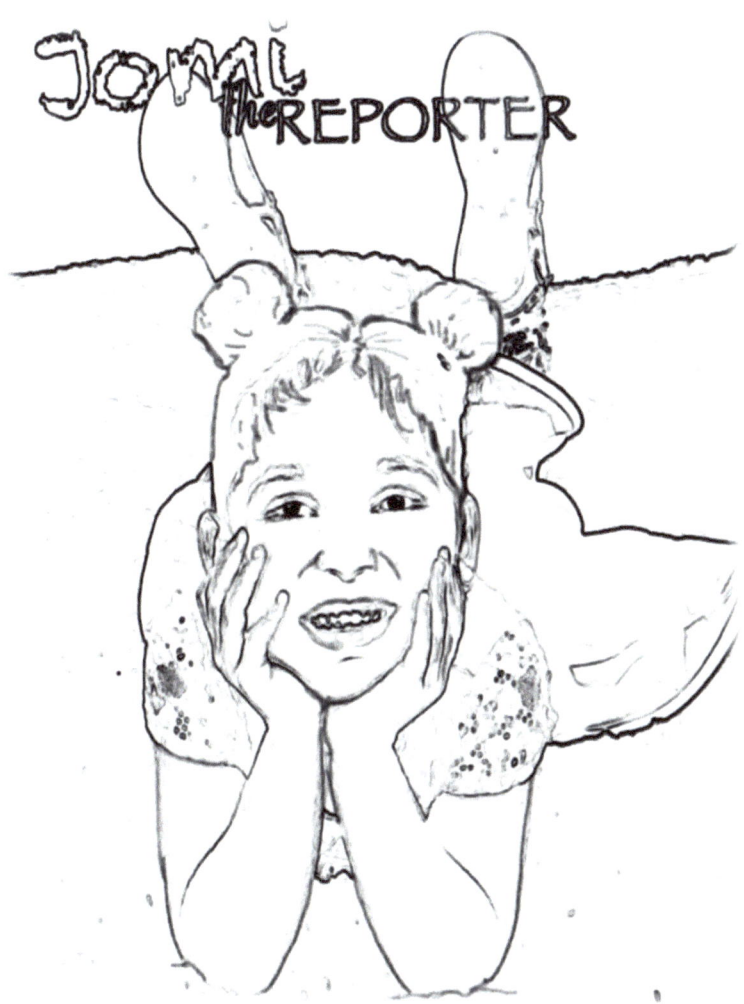

YOU ARE AWESOME   YOU ARE BEAUTIFUL   YOU ARE CHOSEN

27

Jomi The Reporter

YOU ARE AWESOME   YOU ARE BEAUTIFUL   YOU ARE CHOSEN

28

Jomi The Reporter

Dear Friend,

Hi, this is Jomi and I'm writing to you to let you know you are special and unique in so many ways. Just know to love yourself and remember bullying isn't good. I love my little brother Ziki and as special as he is I know he's more than awesome, hey he's my brother, so let's just spread love.

So, if you would like to stay in contact with me just follow me on Facebook at Jomi The Reporter. Please inox me to tell me what other reports you would love to read.

Sincerely

Jomi Yours & Only Reporter

P.S

You could be a reporter too ;)

YOU ARE AWESOME   YOU ARE BEAUTIFUL   YOU ARE CHOSEN

Jomi The Reporter

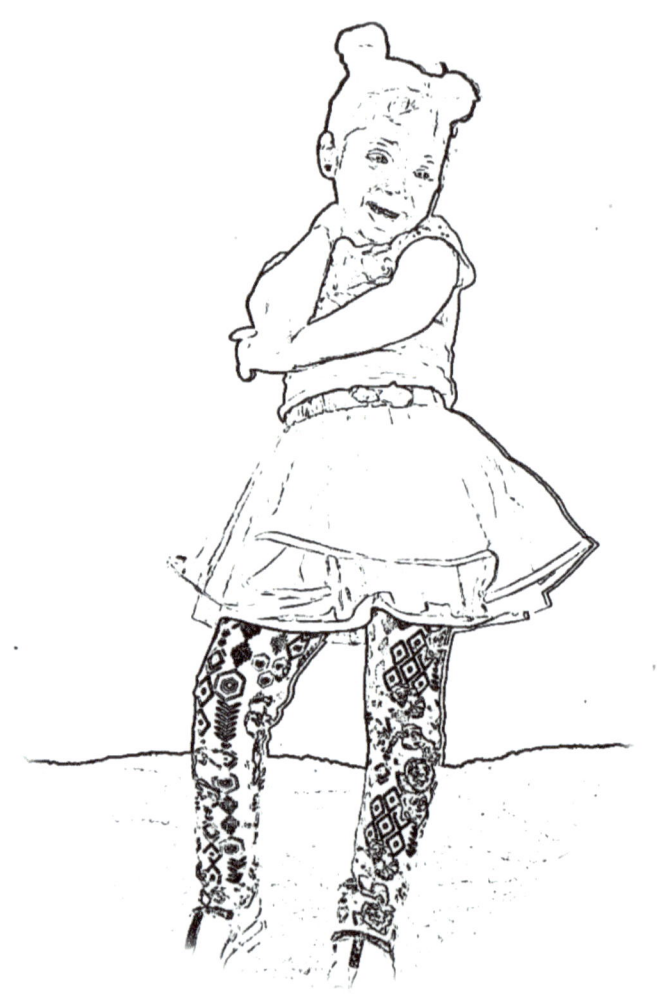

YOU ARE AWESOME   YOU ARE BEAUTIFUL   YOU ARE CHOSEN

30

Jomi The Reporter

Do you know you could write your own book, make your own coloring book and have fun with colors! Awesome, right? So, Start writing your own fun stories down below:

Start Here: _____

_____

_____

_____

_____

_____

_____

_____

_____

_____

_____

YOU ARE AWESOME   YOU ARE BEAUTIFUL   YOU ARE CHOSEN

Jomi The Reporter

_____
_____
_____
_____
_____
_____.
_____

Wow, that's awesome! Someone would love to read that, I know I would. Always know, never stop writing.

YOU ARE AWESOME   YOU ARE BEAUTIFUL   YOU ARE CHOSEN

So go to my Facebook page so you may get more information of what I'm going to be doing next.

Jomi The Reporter

COMING SOON

Jomi The REPORTER
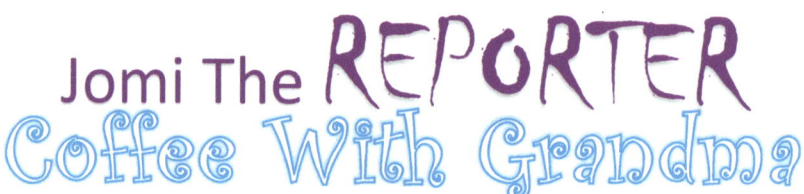

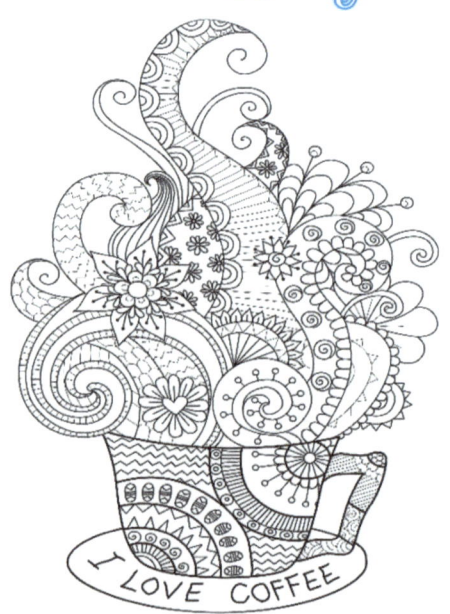

YOU ARE AWESOME   YOU ARE BEAUTIFUL   YOU ARE CHOSEN

34

Jomi The Reporter

YOU ARE AWESOME   YOU ARE BEAUTIFUL   YOU ARE CHOSEN

35

www.ingramcontent.com/pod-product-compliance
Lightning Source LLC
Chambersburg PA
CBHW040358220526

45473CB00018B/513